= *The* =

ECKERT FAMILY
SUMMER COOKBOOK

PEACH, BERRY, TOMATO RECIPES & MORE

= *The* =
ECKERT FAMILY
SUMMER COOKBOOK

PEACH, BERRY, TOMATO RECIPES & MORE

SEVEN GENERATIONS OF RECIPES FROM OUR ORCHARD

REEDY PRESS
St. Louis, Missouri

Reedy Press
PO Box 5131
St. Louis, MO 63139, USA
www.reedypress.com

Library of Congress Control Number: 2013934331

ISBN: 978-1-935806-46-2

Design by Matt Johnson

Printed in the United States of America
13 14 15 16 17   5 4 3 2 1

CONTENTS

INTRODUCTION

Summer's greatest joy is a seemingly endless bounty of delicious fruits and vegetables from the farm. Our family looks forward to sweet and juicy peaches and the extraordinary flavor of homegrown tomatoes. As a result, our dinner tables tend to be filled with salads featuring fresh summer vegetables and simpler recipes that allow the flavors of the summer harvest to shine through.

The summer harvest is versatile, and with seven generations of recipes that have been gathered on the Eckert's farms, *The Eckert Family Summer Cookbook* is our way of sharing time-tested and creative approaches to bringing these foods to your table. The *Summer Cookbook* is the second installment of the Eckert family cookbook series, and all recipes have been modernized and thoroughly tested in our cooking classroom.

Grandma Ella Eckert's baking traditions have kept our strong sense of family alive through the generations. Many of these recipes date back to her collection of cobblers and pies while others are variations. Newer recipes developed in our cooking classroom and in our homes involve a blend of summer vegetables and fresh herbs with refreshing vinaigrettes. With so many delicious summer dishes circling about our family, it was difficult to narrow our selection. This book includes our very favorite and freshest of the summer.

Because our family is also very busy working with the crops on the farm and in our store and restaurant, summer cooking must be simple! We tend to prepare salads to go along with grilled meats. The flavors of locally grown tomatoes, peppers, green beans, and sweet corn are simply unparalleled in these salads. Sweet berries, melons, and peaches are found in many desserts as well as the salads on our tables.

Take advantage of summer's abundance, and the variety that its fruits and vegetables offer. Tomatoes, corn, zucchini, berries, melons, and other summer produce can be transformed into appetizers, desserts, entrées, salads, and even drinks! But nothing beats biting into a fresh peach off the tree as the sun-warmed juices trickle down your chin and a smile spreads across your face.

BREAKFASTS, BREADS, & MUFFINS

Our sales strategy for peaches continues to be the same in our store today as it was generations ago—an endless display of boxes on low tables so guests can see the gorgeous peaches! Young Eckert family members start their business training in the peach sales area where they learn the foundation of our business—high-quality fruit and excellent customer service.

Carole's Peachy Muffins

2 cups sifted flour
1 Tbs. baking powder
¼ tsp. baking soda
⅛ tsp. ground allspice
⅓ cup packed brown sugar
⅓ cup melted butter (5⅓ Tbs.)
1 large egg, beaten
1 cup sour cream
3 Tbs. milk
⅔ cup peeled and chopped peaches

Preheat oven to 400°F. In a large bowl, combine flour, baking powder, baking soda, allspice, and sugar; set aside. In another small bowl, stir butter and egg into milk or sour cream. Add to flour mixture, stirring just enough to moisten. Add peaches and stir until just mixed (batter will be lumpy). Fill greased regular-sized muffin tins ⅔ full (don't use paper liners). Bake for 25 minutes or until golden brown. Cool for 2 to 5 minutes. Remove muffins from tin and allow to fully cool. Makes 12 servings.

--- *From Our Kitchen* ---

To peel peaches quickly, submerge them in boiling water for about 1 minute. Remove the peaches and let them cool slightly before peeling their skins with a paring knife. A soft-skin peeler can be used as a substitute for a paring knife.

Walnutty Peach Bread

3 large eggs
2 cups granulated sugar
2 tsp. vanilla
1 cup vegetable oil
3 cups flour
1 tsp. baking powder
1 tsp. baking soda
1 tsp. salt
1½ tsp. ground cinnamon
2 cups peeled and diced peaches
½ cup finely chopped walnuts

Preheat oven to 350°F. Grease and flour two 8 × 4 loaf pans. In a large bowl, beat eggs lightly. Blend in sugar, vanilla, and oil; set aside. In another small bowl, add flour, baking powder, baking soda, salt, and cinnamon; mix well. Combine dry ingredients with egg mixture and mix just to combine. Stir in peaches and nuts. Pour batter into prepared pans. Bake for about 1 hour or until a tester inserted in the center comes out clean. Remove from oven. Cool 5 to 10 minutes on cooling racks. Loosen sides of cake from pan with knife. Carefully turn over on cooling rack to finish cooling. Makes 10 to 12 servings.

Blackberry Breakfast Bars

FILLING
2 cups fresh blackberries, washed
and drained
2 Tbs. granulated sugar
2 Tbs. water
1 Tbs. lemon juice
½ tsp. ground cinnamon

TO PREPARE FILLING: Preheat oven to 350°F. For filling: In a small saucepan combine berries, sugar, water, lemon juice, and ½ teaspoon cinnamon. Bring to boil. Reduce heat. Simmer, uncovered, for about 8 minutes, stirring frequently. Remove from heat.

TOPPING
1 cup flour
1 cup quick cooking rolled oats
⅔ cup packed brown sugar
¼ tsp. ground cinnamon
⅛ tsp. baking soda
½ cup butter, melted

TO PREPARE TOPPING: In a mixing bowl stir together flour, oats, brown sugar, ¼ teaspoon cinnamon, and baking soda. Stir in melted butter to combine. Set aside 1 cup of the oat mixture for topping. Press remaining oat mixture into an ungreased 9 × 9 × 2 inch pan. Bake crust for 20 to 25 minutes. Spread filling on top of baked crust. Sprinkle with reserved oat mixture. Lightly press oat mixture into filling. Bake for 20 to 25 minutes or until topping is set. Makes 4 to 6 servings.

From Our Farm

Our blackberries are grown on special trellises that allow us to rotate the canes toward the sun. This new growing system creates a wall of fruit at harvest and is much more productive than traditional growing practices.

Best Blueberry Pancakes

1¾ cups flour

2 Tbs. granulated sugar

1 tsp. baking powder

½ tsp. baking soda

½ tsp. salt

¼ tsp. ground nutmeg

2 large eggs

1 cup milk

1 cup sour cream

¼ cup melted butter or vegetable oil, plus extra oil for the pan

½ tsp. vanilla extract

½ tsp. finely grated lemon zest

1½ cups blueberries, rinsed and drained

Eckert's Maple or Blueberry Syrup

In a large mixing bowl combine flour, sugar, baking powder, baking soda, salt, and nutmeg. In a separate large bowl, lightly whisk eggs. Add milk, sour cream, melted butter (or oil), and vanilla extract. Whisk to blend. Make a well in the dry ingredients and pour liquid mixture into it. Vigorously whisk ingredients just until blended (about 10 seconds). Add lemon zest and blueberries and gently fold them into batter. Heat a 12-inch, heavy skillet over medium heat for 3 to 4 minutes. Then pour in enough cooking oil to coat the surface. Using a pot holder to grasp the pan handle with both hands, gently swirl the skillet around to evenly distribute the oil. For each pancake, ladle about ¼ cup of batter onto the hot skillet. Cook pancakes for about 1 to 1½ minutes on the first side, then flip and cook about 1 minute, until the second side is golden brown. Serve pancakes at once. Top with Eckert's Maple Syrup or Blueberry Syrup. Makes 12 pancakes.

Cantaloupe Sorbet

1 medium cantaloupe, washed, peeled, and seeded
2 Tbs. lemon juice
½ cup granulated sugar
¼ cup Eckert's Pure Honey
3 cups milk
½ tsp. vanilla extract

In a blender or food processor fitted with a metal blade, purée cantaloupe and lemon juice. In a large bowl, combine sugar, honey, and milk. Add puréed cantaloupe mixture and vanilla extract. Stir until sugar dissolves, about 2 to 3 minutes. Pour into a 13 × 9 baking pan. Cover, freeze overnight. Soften slightly at room temperature for about 5 to 10 minutes. Spoon into a large bowl. With mixer on low speed, beat until smooth but not melted. Pour into a mold or "freeze-safe" container. Cover; freeze about 4 hours until firm. Unmold or soften about 5 minutes at room temperature for easier scooping. Makes 6 to 8 servings.

STARTERS

— *From Our Family Album* —

Third-generation orchardist, Alvin O. Eckert, shares a moment in the peach orchard located on the Belleville Farm with his three sons, Cornell, Vernon, and Curt. This picture was taken in the 1930s in a young peach orchard. The exact year of Eckert's first peach planting is not known but is estimated to be around 1890. Today, we grow over 200 acres of peaches, which totals over 31,000 trees.

Peach, Prosciutto, and Ricotta Crostini

12 slices Eckert's mini baguette
Olive oil
2-3 Tbs. fresh ricotta
Freshly ground black pepper to taste
4 thin slices of prosciutto
1-2 Tbs. Eckert's Pure Honey
24 slices ripe peaches, peeled and sliced

Preheat oven to 400°F. Brush both sides of sliced bread with olive oil. Bake 4 to 6 minutes. Flip bread. Bake 4 to 6 minutes more. Remove from oven and cool. Spoon fresh ricotta onto each slice of toast and sprinkle with pepper. Tear the prosciutto into feathery pieces and drape a few slices over ricotta-covered toast. Drizzle each with honey and top with 2 peach slices. Makes 12 servings.

Basil-Tomato Bruschetta

1 cup fresh basil, chopped
1 tomato, cored and chopped, peeled or unpeeled
⅓ cup dried fine bread crumbs
4 large garlic cloves, peeled and minced
1 tsp. kosher salt
½ cup olive oil
10-12 slices Eckert's mini baguette
½ cup shredded mozzarella

In bowl, stir together basil, tomato, crumbs, garlic, and salt. Gradually add oil and mix well. (If you make ahead, bring to room temperature before proceeding.) Slice baguette and brush with olive oil. Spoon a bit of mixture on each piece of bread, sprinkle with cheese and broil just until cheese begins to melt. Makes 10 to 12 servings.

Crusty Tomato-Basil Bites

4 medium tomatoes, seeded and chopped

2 Tbs. green or red bell pepper, finely chopped

1 Tbs. red onion, finely chopped

2 garlic cloves, peeled and minced

8 large fresh basil leaves

2 Tbs. olive oil

Salt and ground pepper to taste

1 loaf Eckert's sourdough bread

½ cup shredded Parmesan cheese

In medium bowl combine tomato, bell pepper, onion, and garlic. Stack basil leaves, cut into long, thin strips. Add to tomato mixture with oil. Season with salt and pepper. Cover and let stand at room temperature for 1 to 2 hours to blend flavors. Diagonally cut bread into long, thin slices. Broil or grill on both sides until golden brown, about 1 to 2 minutes. Spoon tomato mixture onto bread slices and sprinkle with Parmesan cheese and additional black pepper. Serve immediately. Makes 14 to 16 servings.

— *From Our Kitchen* —

To remove seeds from a tomato, cut the tomato in half, from side to side. Over the sink, gently scrape the seeds out of the compartments with a small spoon or your fingertip.

Three-Cheese Blackberry Quesadillas with Peach Salsa

4 oz. soft unripened goat cheese

1 pkg (8 oz.) cream cheese, softened

½ cup freshly grated Parmesan

½ cup peeled carrots, grated

8 (6-inch) soft flour tortillas

1⅔ cups fresh or frozen (defrosted) blackberries; well drained, cut in half

Peach Salsa, about 1 cup (recipe on page 81)

Stir together goat cheese, cream cheese, and Parmesan cheese until blended. Add grated carrots; mix well. Spread cheese mixture equally on one side of each tortilla; top with drained blackberries. Fold in half. Cook tortillas, in batches, in a lightly greased, large nonstick skillet over medium-high heat 1 to 2 minutes on each side or until golden brown. Cut into three wedges, and serve with Peach Salsa. Makes 8 servings.

NOTE: Cheese/carrot filling can be made 2 to 3 days ahead of time. Cover and refrigerate. Remove from refrigerator about 1 hour before using so that it is easier to spread.

--- *From Our Kitchen* ---

To soften peaches quickly, allow them to rest on your kitchen counter for a day or two. To slow their softening, keep them in the refrigerator for up to 1 week. Peaches are best when bought often and used quickly.

Great Zukes Pizza Bites

1 medium zucchini
3 Tbs. pizza sauce
2 Tbs. tomato paste
¼ tsp. dried or ¾ tsp. fresh oregano
¾ cup (3 oz.) mozzarella cheese
¼ cup shredded Parmesan cheese
8 slices pitted black olives
8 slices pepperoni

Set oven rack 4 inches from heat, and preheat broiler. Trim off ends of zucchini and cut into 16 (¼-inch thick) diagonal pieces. Place on a nonstick baking sheet. Combine pizza sauce, tomato paste, and oregano in a small bowl and mix well. Spread teaspoon of sauce over each zucchini slice. Combine cheeses in small bowl. Top each zucchini slice with 1 tablespoon of cheese mixture, pressing down into sauce. Place 1 olive slice on each of 8 zucchini slices. Place 1 folded pepperoni slice on each remaining zucchini slice. Broil 3 minutes or until cheese is melted. Serve immediately. Makes 8 servings.

Blueberry and Peach Compote

3 Tbs. Eckert's Pure Honey
¾ tsp. finely grated lime peel
1 tsp. fresh lime juice
Pinch of salt
3 firm, ripe peaches, halved
1 cup fresh blueberries or
    blackberries, cleaned

In a small, ½-quart saucepan combine honey, grated lime, lime juice, and salt. Cook over medium heat, stirring frequently, until well-combined and smooth, about 1 minute. Let cool slightly. Cut each peach half into wedges ¼- to ½-inch thick and cut crosswise into halves or thirds. Put peaches and berries in a bowl and drizzle the warm honey mixture over top; toss gently. Serve in individual glass bowls or martini glasses. Makes 6 servings.

—— *From Our Family Album* ——

The entry-level position for all Eckert children has remained the same year after year—folding 2-quart pans (boxes) for our Fancy-grade peaches. Although it may sound boring to fold hundreds of flat pieces of cardboard into boxes, 2-quart pan folding can be an exciting introduction to "going to work."

Chorizo Quesadillas

½ lb. Eckert's Fresh Chorizo Sausage (2 links)

10 flour or corn tortillas (6-inch)

1 red bell pepper, diced

2 ears corn, kernels removed from the cob

1 green bell pepper, diced

2 cups shredded mild cheddar cheese

Remove sausage from the casing and sauté until fully cooked, allow to cool a few minutes. Place 5 tortillas on a work surface. Dividing evenly, scatter chorizo, bell pepper, and corn over each, leaving ¼-inch border all around. Sprinkle cheese over each and top with remaining tortillas. Press lightly to seal. Place 1 quesadilla between 2 paper towels, top with another quesadilla and another paper towel. Microwave the 2 stacked quesadillas on high for 2 minutes or until cheese has melted. Carefully unstack quesadillas (they will be very hot), and remove paper towels. Place on a platter. Repeat with remaining quesadillas. Cut each quesadilla into 4 wedges and serve with guacamole.

Eckert's Peach-Fresh Basil Iced Tea

8 cups peeled and finely crushed ripe peaches

2 family-size tea bags

1 cup loosely packed fresh cinnamon basil or sweet basil leaves, cleaned

About ½ cup Eckert's Pure Honey or ⅔ cup granulated sugar

Crushed ice

Fresh peach slices for garnish

In a stainless saucepan, over medium heat, cook peaches until soft and juicy, about 5 to 6 minutes. Set aside to cool slightly. In another pan, bring 8 cups of water to a boil. Add tea bags and basil; allow to steep 6 to 8 minutes. Remove and discard tea bags and basil. Add honey or sugar, stirring until dissolved. Set aside. Return to the peaches, purée until smooth using a blender or food processor. Add this mixture to the basil tea liquid. Stir. Adjust sweetness.

Serve over crushed ice. Garnish side of glass with a fresh peach slice. Makes about 3 quarts, or 12 servings (8 oz. each).

From Our Kitchen

To keep basil fresh and fragrant after cutting or purchasing, do not store it in the refrigerator. Simply place the cut ends in a jar of water on your countertop.

Peach Daiquiri

1 medium peach
1 oz. fresh lime juice
1-2 tsp. granulated sugar
3 oz. rum
1 cup cracked ice

Mix all ingredients in a blender until smooth. Serve immediately. Makes 1 serving.

Cherry Peach Sangria

¼ cup granulated sugar
¼ cup brandy
3 cups Rainier cherries, pitted and halved
1 bottle chilled white wine
1 cup chilled club soda
1 large peach, peeled and sliced thin

Combine sugar and brandy in a pitcher and stir until sugar dissolves. Add cherries and wine and refrigerate for 8 to 24 hours. Just before serving, add club soda and peach slices. Makes 6 servings.

Berry Mix-Up

¼ cup crushed ice

2 Tbs. blueberries (about 10)

½ small peach, chopped

1 scoop (about ¼ cup) Eckert's Frozen Vanilla Custard

½ to 1 tsp. Eckert's Pure Honey

Place all ingredients into blender. Blend until mixture is smooth, about 1 minute. Makes 1 serving.

From Our Farm

Fresh produce is a way of life for the Eckert family so we are always looking for ways to extend the harvest season. Recently we have begun experimenting with "high tunnel" greenhouses to create an environment for earlier plantings and an extended harvest of tomatoes and berries.

Misty Melon Cooler

2 cups very ripe cantaloupe, peeled, seeded, and diced
1 cup orange juice
3 Tbs. granulated sugar
Eckert's Frozen Vanilla Custard

Place melon chunks on a plate and place it in the freezer until fruit is firm but not frozen solid, about 20 to 30 minutes. In a blender, purée the melon chunks with the orange juice and sugar until mixture is smooth. Add custard and blend mixture until smooth, about 1 to 2 minutes. Divide cooler among four glasses and serve. Makes four (8 oz.) servings.

Peaches 'n Cream Smoothie

1 large ripe peach, sliced
½ banana, cut into 3 pieces
½ cup whole milk
½ cup Eckert's Frozen Vanilla Custard

In a blender, purée peach and banana. Add whole milk. Blend until a smooth texture is formed. Add custard and blend until smooth. Makes 1 serving.

—— *From Our Farm* ——

Peach trees, about a half inch in diameter, are transplanted into the orchard in early spring and they grow very fast. They will produce enough peaches to be harvested in the third year after being transplanted, and they will continue to be productive for up to 15 years.

SALADS

In the 1930s, our peach-packing line was humble yet highly effective at sizing fruit. Hand-picked peaches were transferred from wooden crates and baskets to the sizing belt where careful hands would sort out the damaged and overripe fruit. Today, our packing line is computerized, and we harvest peaches in plastic totes. But all our peaches are still harvested by hand, quality checked with careful eyes, and gently placed into the same handled baskets we have used for eighty years for our guests to carry home.

Tomato Salad with Dressing

1 cup fresh chopped tomatoes, peeled or unpeeled
⅓ cup red wine vinegar
1 dash Worcestershire sauce
2 tsp. Dijon mustard
1 Tbs. fresh basil, minced
1 Tbs. fresh thyme, minced

Place tomatoes, vinegar, Worcestershire sauce, mustard, basil, and thyme in a small bowl; mix thoroughly. Cover and refrigerate. Bring to room temperature before serving. Makes 4 servings.

Summer Fruit and Greens Salad with Poppyseed Dressing

DRESSING
3 Tbs. red wine vinegar
⅓ cup granulated sugar
1 tsp. dry mustard
¾ tsp. kosher salt
⅓ cup vegetable oil
1 Tbs. poppy seeds

SALAD
5-6 cups fresh salad greens
1½ cups cantaloupe, diced
1½ cups fresh blueberries
2 large peaches, peeled and sliced

Blend all dressing ingredients. Place greens on a platter. Mix fruit and dressing together in a large bowl. Pour on top of greens and serve. Makes 6 servings.

Chicken and Peach Summer Salad for Two

2 large peaches, peeled and sliced

2 tsp. lemon juice

Romaine lettuce leaves, torn into bite-size pieces (approximately 4 cups)

1 cup diced cooked chicken breast or deli meat

2 green onions, cleaned and sliced

2 medium tomatoes, chopped and seeded

2 hard-cooked eggs, chopped

2 slices crisply cooked bacon, crumbled

1 avocado, peeled and diced

Sweet Curry Dressing to taste (recipe follows)

Sprinkle peaches with lemon juice. Line large individual salad bowls with lettuce. In a separate bowl, mix chicken and onion with enough Sweet Curry Dressing to moisten. Arrange peaches in center of lettuce. Top with a mound of chicken mixture. Arrange tomato, egg, bacon, and avocado around edges. Serve cold with Sweet Curry Dressing on side. Serves 2.

Sweet Curry Dressing

½ cup sour cream or mayonnaise

2 Tbs. + ¼ tsp. milk

¼ tsp. curry powder

⅛ tsp. salt

1 tsp. wine vinegar

1-2 tsp. Eckert's Pure Honey

In a bowl, blend together sour cream and milk. Whisk in curry powder, salt, vinegar, and honey to taste. Serves 2.

Peach and Goat Cheese Salad with Honey Vinaigrette

1 Tbs. balsamic vinegar (white or dark)

2 tsp. fresh lemon juice

2 tsp. Eckert's Pure Honey

¼ tsp. kosher salt

3 Tbs. olive oil

4 ripe peaches, peeled and sliced

1 (5 oz.) package baby lettuce mix (6 cups)

½ cup crumbled goat cheese (chèvre)

½ cup toasted almonds or candied pecans

Coarsely ground black pepper to taste

Whisk together vinegar, lemon juice, honey, and salt. Then add oil in a stream, whisking until thickened, about 1 to 2 minutes. Divide lettuce among 8 salad plates. Top with peaches, goat cheese, and nuts. Drizzle with dressing and sprinkle with pepper. Serve immediately. Makes 8 servings.

From Our Farm

Although peaches get softer and juicier, they do not get any sweeter after they are picked. That is why we let them ripen on the tree to maximum sweetness before we harvest them.

Garden Bean and Potato Salad with Balsamic Vinaigrette

VINAIGRETTE

¼ cup balsamic vinegar (white or dark)
2 Tbs. Dijon mustard
2 Tbs. fresh lemon juice
1 tsp. salt
Dash of Worcestershire sauce
1 garlic clove, minced
½ cup olive oil

SALAD

1½ lbs. small, round red potatoes, peeled if desired
¾ lb. fresh green beans, trimmed
1 small red onion, diced
¼ cup chopped fresh basil

TO PREPARE VINAIGRETTE: In a medium bowl, whisk all dressing ingredients except oil until well combined. Gradually stream in oil while whisking until emulsified.

TO PREPARE SALAD: Arrange potatoes in a steamer basket over boiling water; cover and steam 20 minutes or until tender. Place potatoes in a large serving bowl, quarter when cool enough to handle. Arrange beans in steamer basket over boiling water; cover and steam 10 minutes or until crisp-tender. Drain. Add beans, onion and basil to potatoes. Drizzle Balsamic Vinaigrette on potato mixture and toss gently. Serve immediately. To serve later, cover and refrigerate potatoes and beans. Add dressing before serving. Makes 6 to 8 servings.

Summer Succotash
with Lemon-Honey Dressing

LEMON-HONEY DRESSING
13 Tbs. olive oil
1½ Tbs. fresh lemon juice
1 tsp. Eckert's Pure Honey
½ small red onion, minced
Salt and pepper to taste

SUCCOTASH
¾ lb. green beans, trimmed and cut in half
1 cup corn kernels (2 ears)
½ lb. lima beans, fresh or frozen (defrosted)—optional
2 Tbs. chopped fresh or 3 Tbs. dried basil

TO PREPARE DRESSING: Stir the oil, lemon juice, honey, red onion, salt, and pepper together in a small bowl.

TO PREPARE SUCCOTASH: Bring 2½ quarts of water to a boil in a large saucepan. Add 1 teaspoon salt to water and add green beans; cook for 1 minute. Add corn and lima beans and cook until tender, about 5 minutes. Drain vegetables into a colander and rinse under cold running water until cool. Drain vegetables well and transfer to a serving bowl. Toss vegetables with dressing to coat evenly. Stir in basil and season with additional salt and pepper to taste. Makes 4 servings.

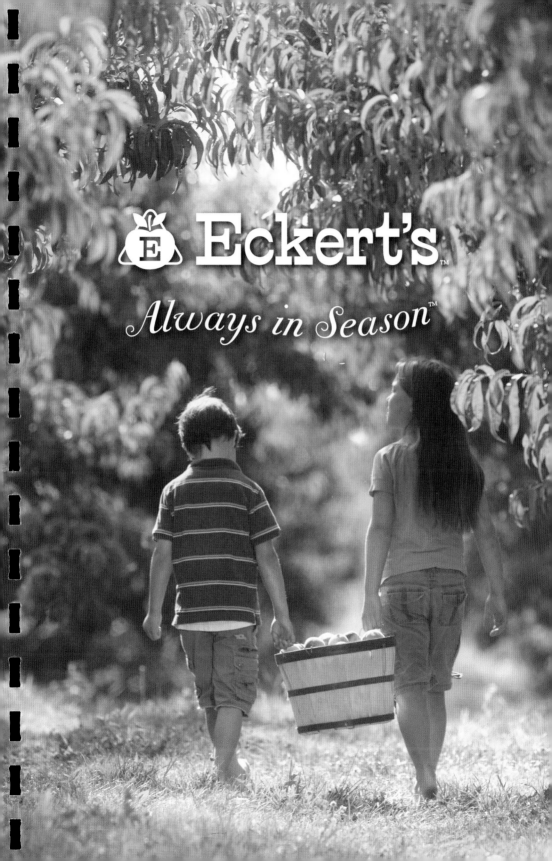

Peaches—the Eckert Way

The Eckert family selects only the best-tasting peach varieties to plant on our farms. Many of the varieties that are available are produced with an emphasis on the fruit looking great rather than it tasting great. However, we always opt for the best-tasting peaches. Eckert's peach trees are not allowed to produce fruit for the first several years so they can invest all their energy in growing roots and branches to support the largest and sweetest fruit possible. Every decision we make is to deliver the best-tasting peach possible!

PRUNING

Our peach trees are pruned by hand, all 35,000 of them. Our crew has been trained to identify the best-producing shoots and individually remove the rest. This allows more sunlight into the trees, resulting in sweeter, better-tasting fruit.

THINNING PEACHES

Eckert's peach trees are thinned three times every year to maximize fruit size. We begin this process at bloom, which is the most important time to thin if you want the largest, best-tasting peaches. We thin two more times during the growing season, ultimately removing peaches by hand one at a time, to ensure the largest, highest-quality fruit.

HYDRO COOL

Eckert's peaches are harvested at the peak of ripeness. This results in the best-tasting and the softest fruit. Since we typically harvest fruit on the hottest days of the summer, heat must be removed from the peach as soon as it is harvested. All peaches pass under a cold shower of 34°F water for

two minutes. This cools the fruit about 20 degrees and stops the ripening process. Eckert's is the only farm in the Midwest that uses this type of hydro cooling, and it is one of the reasons we believe our peaches are the best in the world.

TREE RIPENED

Peaches do not get any sweeter once they are picked. They do get softer and juicier, but no more sugar is produced. We let our peaches ripen to maximum sweetness before we harvest them—that is why Eckert peaches taste so good.

Our peaches should be softened at room temperature for a day or two. This actually reduces the acidity, therefore making the peach taste sweeter.

PEACH MEASURING HINTS

1 pound equals 3 medium-size peaches, 2 cups sliced peaches, or 1 cup pulp

1¼ pounds yields 1 pint frozen or canned peaches

VARIETIES

There are two types of peaches: clingstone and freestone.

Clingstone: Generally speaking, the early ripening peaches are clingstone, which means that the "meat" of the peach sticks (clings) to the seed (stone). Because they do not come free from the stone, they are not the most desirable peaches to freeze or can, but they are nice to eat out of your hand just like an apple.

Freestone: These peaches release easily (come free) from their seed (stone). We grow approximately 30 varieties of yellow freestone peaches, but since many of them are similar, we have grouped them together into some primary varieties: Red Haven, Cresthaven, and Loring.

CANTALOUPE

SELECTING—Select cantaloupes with a musky, sweet smell. The end opposite of the stem should yield slightly to pressure.

WATERMELON

SELECTING—Melons should be heavy for their size and have a yellow spot on their underside where they ripened in the sun. They should be firm and symmetrical.

STORING MELONS—Store whole melons in the refrigerator for up to a week. Cut melon should be refrigerated in a covered container and kept 3 to 4 days.

BLACKBERRIES

Blackberries are best when used immediately, but may be refrigerated for 1 to 2 days. Wash berries and pat dry. Place 1 to 2 layers on a shallow plate and cover with a paper towel. Do not heap berries on top of one another as this increases the risk of damage, and do not soak berries in water.

Blackberry Jam

2 cups fresh blackberries (about 1 qt. berries)

4 cups granulated sugar

1 package powdered pectin

1 cup water

Sort and wash fully ripe berries. Drain. Place berries in a large mixing bowl and mash with a fork. Add sugar to mashed berries and allow to stand for 20 minutes, stirring occasionally. Dissolve pectin in water and boil for 1 minute. Add pectin solution to berry and sugar mixture; stir for 2 minutes. Pour about 1 cup of berry mixture into pint-size freezer containers (makes about 5 cups), leaving ½ inch of headspace. Cover with a lid and let stand at room temperature for 24 hours.

Store the jam in the refrigerator or freezer. Jam will last about 3 weeks in the refrigerator and up to a year in the freezer. Once the container is opened, the jam should be stored in the refrigerator and used within a few days. Do not store at room temperature after the initial 24-hour "setting-up" stage.

BLUEBERRIES

Blueberries are known for being packed with nutrition. They reach their maximum nutritional value when eaten fresh, so enjoying them on top of your cereal, yogurt, or salad is a great way to ensure you get all the health benefits blueberries offer.

SELECTING—Look for firm, dry, plump, and smooth-skinned berries. Size isn't an indicator of maturity but color is—berries should be deep purple-blue to blue-black. Reddish berries aren't ripe.

STORING—Refrigerate berries right away. Don't wash berries until right before eating as washing will remove the bloom that protects the berries' skins from degradation. Store ripe blueberries in a covered container in the refrigerator for up to 5 days.

Freezing Berries

Since berries are so seasonal, freezing is an easy way to lengthen the time you get to enjoy them. Our suggestion for freezing them:

Wash and gently pat berries dry with paper towels. Spread on a rimmed baking sheet lined with waxed paper in a single layer. Freeze about 6 to 8 hours or until the berries are solidly frozen. Place frozen berries in airtight containers or plastic zipper freezer bags. Label with date.

CORN

SELECTING—Squeeze the ear to make sure the kernels are closely spaced, firm, and round. Look for a grassy-green, tightly wrapped husk. The silk should be glossy and pale yellow, the stem moist.

STORING—You can store corn in the refrigerator for a day or two. Do not strip off the husks and silk until right before cooking.

How to Remove Kernels from the Cob

An easy way to remove corn kernels from the cob is by using a bundt pan. Stand the shucked corn cob upright, with the tip of the cob placed in the center hole of the bundt pan.

Holding the cob steady, use a sharp knife and make long downward strokes on the cob, separating the kernels from the cob. This will catch the kernels and keep them from flying all over your counter and the hole in the bundt pan helps hold the corn cob steady.

Perfectly Prepared Corn on the Cob

An easy way to prepare corn on the cob (and the BEST way—we think) is by microwaving the corn in the husks. We usually figure between 1½ to 2 minutes per ear of corn (up to your liking on crunchiness). Let the corn cool for about 1 minute, then shuck it—the silks comes off beautifully. Be warned though—the corn is very hot—you might want to use a pot holder to help do this. We recommend only microwaving 4 ears of corn at a time.

If you like to husk your corn before microwaving, you can do that and put the corn in a plastic bag. Microwave the corn the same amount of time and still just heat 4 to 5 ears of corn at a time.

PEPPERS

SELECTING—Red bell peppers are simply mature green peppers; yellow and orange bell peppers are different, sweeter varieties. Keep an eye out for firm peppers with shiny, wrinkle-free skins.

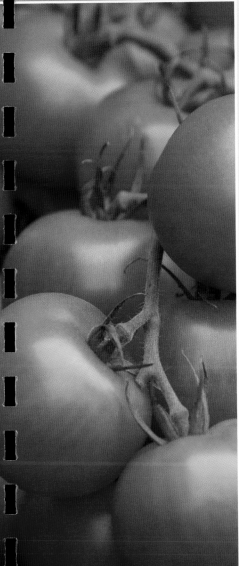

STORING—Peppers should be kept refrigerated in a plastic bag. Red and yellow peppers last for about 5 days, while green peppers keep for about a week.

TOMATOES

SELECTING—Select tomatoes that are deeply colored and firm with a little give and that have a sweet, woody smell.

STORING—Tomatoes should be stored at room temperature and used within a few days. Tomatoes should NEVER be refrigerated or set in the sun.

Freezing Tomatoes

While not absolutely necessary, blanching your tomatoes first will ensure a fresher taste upon defrosting. The defrosted tomatoes work best in sauces or stews. Tomatoes should be frozen while they are still ripe or slightly immature. They should be firm with no soft spots or bruises.

Instructions

Wash tomatoes under running warm water. Remove any stems. Next, fill a large bowl with cold water. Then cut a tiny "x" on the bottom of each tomato with a paring knife, cutting lightly through the skin only. Bring a pot of water to boil. Submerge two to three tomatoes at a time into the boiling water and boil them for 30 to 45 seconds. Remove the tomatoes with a slotted spoon and plunge immediately into a cold-water bath to stop the cooking process. Peel away the tomato skins using the edge of a paring knife (the skins should slide off easily). Let your tomatoes sit in a colander for a few minutes to drain any excess water. Place the tomatoes into freezer bags. You can freeze them whole, in halves, or in quarters. You can also remove the excess seeds and water from inside the tomato. Squeeze the freezer bags (avoiding the tomatoes) before sealing to allow excess air to escape. Place your tomatoes in the freezer. Frozen tomatoes stay good for three to four months.

Eating Peaches—the Eckert Way

You will find peach pies, peach cakes, and many other special peach desserts on the tables of the Eckert families, but this recipe is the one used over and over all peach season long. We never get tired of eating those magnificent peaches!

1. As many peaches as you can eat
2. As much sugar as you care to add (usually not too much)
3. A little lemon juice or ascorbic acid (to prevent browning)

Peel and slice the peaches into a bowl. Sprinkle sugar and ascorbic acid over the peaches and allow to sit and "draw juice" (30 to 45 minutes). Eat them just like that or over ice cream, cereal, half and half, sponge cake, with whipped cream . . . the options are endless, but the results are absolutely delicious!

Peachy Sangria

2 bottles of Montelle Peachy Wine

24 oz. orange juice

24 oz. grapefruit soda or white soda

10 Eckert's peaches, sliced

1 lb. white grapes, frozen

1 lemon, thinly sliced

Combine wine, orange juice, peaches, and sliced lemon in a large pitcher. Refrigerate overnight. When ready to serve, add soda and frozen grapes. Frozen grapes will keep the drink cold without diluting the flavor. (It is easy to cut this recipe in half, too!)

Summer Orzo Salad with Red Wine Vinaigrette

RED WINE VINAIGRETTE
½ cup red wine vinegar
¼ cup fresh lemon juice
2-3 tsp. Eckert's Pure Honey
2 tsp. salt
¾ tsp. freshly ground black pepper
1 cup olive oil

ORZO SALAD
4 cups chicken broth
1½ cups uncooked orzo
1 (15-oz.) can garbanzo beans, drained and rinsed
1½ cups red cherry or grape tomatoes, halved
1 cup peeled and diced cucumbers
¾ cup finely chopped red onions
2 Tbs. chopped fresh basil leaves
2 Tbs. chopped fresh lemon thyme or lemon verbena

TO PREPARE VINAIGRETTE: Mix vinegar, lemon juice, honey, salt, and pepper in a blender or shaker. Whisk in oil gradually. Season vinaigrette, to taste, with more salt and pepper if desired.

TO PREPARE ORZO SALAD: Pour broth into a large, heavy saucepan. Cover pan and bring broth to a boil over high heat. Stir in orzo. Cook until orzo is tender but still firm to the bite, stirring frequently, about 7 minutes. Drain orzo through a strainer. Transfer orzo to a large, wide bowl and toss until it cools slightly (can put in refrigerator to speed up the process). Toss orzo with beans, tomatoes, cucumbers, onion, herbs. Add vinaigrette to orzo salad to your taste. Season salad with salt and pepper and serve at room temperature or chilled. Cover and refrigerate any remaining dressing for another salad. Makes about 1¾ cups dressing. Makes 5 to 6 servings.

Confetti Salad with Ranch Dressing

RANCH DRESSING
¼ cup buttermilk
¼ cup sour cream
1 Tbs. apple cider vinegar
3 Tbs. olive oil
2 Tbs. chopped, fresh chives
⅛ tsp. salt, or more, to taste
1 large red bell pepper, cut into 1-inch rings (garnish)

SALAD
1 cup couscous, uncooked
1½ cups boiling water
¾ cup diced zucchini
¾ cup diced red bell pepper
¾ cup fresh corn kernels (from about 1-2 ears)
½ cup diced celery
¼ cup chopped fresh parsley
Salt and pepper to taste

TO PREPARE DRESSING: Combine buttermilk, sour cream, vinegar, and olive oil in a small bowl and vigorously whisk mixture. Stir in chives and salt.

TO PREPARE SALAD: Measure couscous into a medium bowl. Stir in boiling water. Cover bowl with plastic wrap and set aside until water is absorbed (about 10 minutes). Fluff couscous with a fork and let it cool at room temperature. Add zucchini, bell pepper, corn, celery, and parsley to couscous and toss mixture well.

Pour enough dressing over couscous and vegetables to coat lightly, then toss again. Season salad with salt and pepper. Place a pepper ring on each serving plate and fill with salad. Makes 6 to 8 servings.

Peach Tomato Motz

2 medium homegrown tomatoes, cored and sliced
½-1 tsp. kosher salt
½ red onion, thinly sliced
1 tsp. to ½ Tbs. granulated sugar
2 medium peaches, peeled, sliced from pit
2-4 Tbs. olive oil
1-2 Tbs. apple cider vinegar
8 oz. fresh mozzarella cheese, sliced

Layer tomato slices on a rimmed platter. Salt. Top with thin slices of red onion. Sprinkle sugar across platter. Top with peach slices. Drizzle with olive oil and cider vinegar. Top with mozzarella slices. Makes 4 servings.

Fresh Summer Corn Salad with Creamy Vinaigrette

CREAMY VINAIGRETTE
¼ cup balsamic vinegar
¼ cup mayonnaise
¼ cup olive oil
1 clove of garlic, minced
¾ tsp. Italian herbs or seasoning

SALAD
4-5 ears of corn in husk (2½ cups, cooked)
1 small red onion, halved and sliced
2-3 medium tomatoes, seeded and chopped
1 small zucchini, finely chopped
¼ to ½ tsp. kosher salt, optional

TO PREPARE VINAIGRETTE: Combine vinegar, mayonnaise, olive oil, garlic, and herbs in small bowl. Whisk to emulsify or blend; set aside.

TO PREPARE SALAD: Microwave ears of corn in husk for approximately 2 minutes per ear (if cooking 4 ears, cook for 7½ to 8 minutes). Husk corn under cold running water. Cut corn from the ears. Combine all vegetables in a large bowl and drizzle with dressing. Add salt if desired. Makes 6 to 8 servings.

Grilled Summer Salad with Blue Cheese Vinaigrette

VINAIGRETTE

2 Tbs. sherry vinegar

7 Tbs. olive oil

½ tsp. kosher salt

Fresh ground pepper

2 Tbs. blue cheese, softened

1 tsp. finely chopped fresh thyme leaves

1 small tomato, seeded and diced

SALAD

1 (5 oz.) package mix greens (6 cups)

1 red bell pepper, grilled

4 large portabella caps, grilled

1 large red onion, grilled

1 cup fresh corn, cut from cob (2 ears corn, grilled)

In a small bowl, whisk together vinegar, oil, salt, pepper, and blue cheese. With fork, mash cheese against the side of the bowl. Add thyme and tomato. Stir vigorously. Mound the greens on a platter or individual plates. Thinly slice peppers and portabellas and place on the greens. Separate onion into rings and top with vegetables. Cut corn off the cobs and sprinkle on top. Drizzle dressing over top. Makes 4 servings.

Tomato and Watermelon Salad

DRESSING

2 Tbs. balsamic vinegar (white or dark)

1 Tbs. fresh lemon juice

½ cup olive oil

1 Tbs. chopped fresh tarragon leaves (optional)

SALAD

2 tomatoes, stemmed, washed, and dried

2 cups (1 pint) cherry tomatoes, stemmed, washed and dried and cut in half

Salt and pepper to taste

1-2 tsp. granulated sugar

1 Tbs. chopped fresh tarragon leaves

6 oz. cold watermelon, rind removed, seeded and cut into bite-size cubes

TO PREPARE DRESSING: In a bowl, whisk together balsamic vinegar, lemon juice, and olive oil. Add tarragon.

TO PREPARE SALAD: Cut larger tomatoes into slices on baking sheet. Arrange all tomatoes in a single layer, flesh side up. Season with salt, pepper, and sugar. Sprinkle tarragon leaves across tomatoes. Drizzle tomatoes with about half of dressing. To serve the dressed tomatoes, arrange down the length of 6 rectangular plates. Drizzle with remaining dressing and top with watermelon cubes. Serve immediately. Makes 6 servings.

Blackberry Spinach Salad

3 cups baby spinach, washed and rinsed

2 cups (1 pint) fresh blackberries, washed

6 oz. crumbled feta cheese

1 green onion, sliced

2 cups (1 pint) cherry tomatoes, halved

¼ cup finely chopped walnuts

In a large bowl, toss together baby spinach, blackberries, feta cheese, cherry tomatoes, green onion, and walnuts. Drizzle with Eckert's Apple Cider Vinaigrette. Makes 4 servings.

Cherry Tomato and Feta Salad

8 cups (4 pints) grape or cherry tomatoes, halved

1½ cups small, diced red onion (2 small onions)

¼ cup white balsamic vinegar

6 Tbs. olive oil

1 Tbs. kosher salt

1 tsp. freshly ground black pepper

¼ cup chopped, fresh basil leaves

8 oz. feta cheese, crumbled

Place tomatoes in a large bowl. Add onion, vinegar, olive oil, salt, pepper, and basil and toss well. Gently fold feta into salad and serve at room temperature. Makes 12 to 14 servings.

Blueberry, Cantaloupe, and Blue Cheese Salad

DRESSING

2 tsp. grated lime zest

3 Tbs. lime juice (fresh only)

1 Tbs. Eckert's Pure Honey

¼ cup finely chopped, fresh basil

¼ cup finely chopped, fresh parsley

½ tsp. pepper

Salt to taste

¼ cup olive oil

SALAD

2 cups (1 pint) blueberries

2 small cantaloupes, halved, use melon baller to scoop

1 cup blue cheese, crumbled (can use Gorgonzola)

½ cup toasted pecans, chopped

TO PREPARE DRESSING: In a small bowl, combine lime zest, lime juice, honey, basil, and parsley. Whisk in oil and add salt and pepper to taste.

TO PREPARE SALAD: Combine salad ingredients in a large bowl. Drizzle dressing over salad ingredients and toss lightly. Serve immediately. Makes 6½ cups.

From Our Farm

Our blueberry plants are grown in special soil because they prefer acidic conditions. We amended the soil with peat moss before planting, and we mulch with wood chips to insulate the shallow roots.

Melon and Prosciutto Salad with Parmesan

3 cups cubed honeydew melon
3 cups cubed cantaloupe
2 Tbs. sliced fresh mint
1 tsp. fresh lemon juice
¼ tsp. freshly ground black pepper
2 oz. prosciutto, cut into strips
½ cup shaved Parmesan cheese

Combine honeydew, cantaloupe, sliced mint, lemon juice, and pepper, tossing gently. Arrange melon mixture on a serving platter. Arrange prosciutto evenly over melon mixture; sprinkle with Parmesan. Garnish with cracked black pepper and fresh mint sprigs, if desired. Makes 6 servings.

Judy's Creamy Tomato and Cucumber Salad

¼ cup regular mayonnaise
2 Tbs. white vinegar
2 tsp. granulated sugar
2 homegrown tomatoes, cored and sliced
1 large homegrown cucumber, peeled and thinly sliced
1 medium sweet onion, finely sliced (optional)
Kosher salt to taste

In a small bowl, make dressing by whisking together first 3 ingredients; set aside. Place tomato slices on a platter or large plate, salt to taste. Top tomatoes with cucumbers and onions if using. Dollop dressing on top and toss. Allow to rest and draw juices for 10 to 15 minutes. Serve immediately. Makes 3 to 4 servings.

NOTE: Do not substitute light mayonnaise.

SIDES

The Eckert family's retail endeavor began as a seasonal roadside stand in Belleville. In the early 1900s, Alvin O. Eckert operated what would blossom into more than one hundred years in retail. On our one hundredth-year anniversary in retail, we built a new Country Store in Belleville.

Sweet Lime Watermelon Bites

½ cup freshly squeezed lime juice (about 4 medium limes)
½ cup Eckert's Pure Honey
Watermelon, cut in ½-inch chunks
Mint sprigs, for garnish

Place lime juice and honey in a saucepan over low heat or on the side burners of a grill. Bring to a boil and let boil for 2 minutes. Remove from heat and allow to cool. Place watermelon chunks on a large platter and drizzle with the lime syrup and garnish with mint. Makes 4 servings.

Very Sherry Cherry Tomatoes

2 Tbs. olive oil
3 large garlic cloves, finely chopped
1 small onion, finely chopped
2 cups (1 pint) cherry or grape tomatoes
2 Tbs. sherry vinegar or balsamic vinegar
1 Tbs. granulated sugar
½ tsp. crushed red pepper flakes
½ tsp. salt

Preheat oven to 375°F. Heat a skillet to medium-high heat. Add olive oil, garlic, and onions. Sauté 2 to 3 minutes, then add tomatoes. Turn tomatoes to coat. Add vinegar, sugar, red pepper, and salt to taste. Toss to coat tomatoes. Roast in oven 18 to 20 minutes or until soft and browned. Makes about 1 cup.

Roasted Tomatoes Gratin

4 medium tomatoes, cut in half
Ground black pepper
¼ cup dry bread crumbs
¼ cup grated Parmesan cheese
2 Tbs. butter, melted
1 tsp. minced garlic

Preheat oven to 450°F. Line a baking sheet with aluminum foil. Place tomato halves, cut side up, on the prepared baking sheet. Season with salt and pepper, set aside. In a small bowl, combine bread crumbs, Parmesan cheese, butter, and garlic. Spoon over tomatoes. Roast tomatoes for 10 to 12 minutes or until bread crumb mixture is golden brown. Makes 4 servings.

——— *From Our Farm* ———

We plant tomatoes several times in the late spring and early summer to ensure an extended harvest season. In an ideal year, we will harvest tomatoes from June through September.

Zucchini Pasta with Basil Pesto

BASIL PESTO

1 cup packed fresh basil leaves

⅓ cup vegetable broth

½ cup grated Asiago cheese, divided

2 large garlic cloves, quartered

2 tsp. olive oil

ZUCCHINI PASTA

3 yellow summer squashes, about ¾ lb. total

3 peeled zucchini, about ¾ lb. total

¼ cup chopped shallot

Salt and freshly ground pepper to taste

TO PREPARE PESTO: In a blender or food processor, combine basil, broth, ¼ cup Asiago cheese, garlic, and olive oil. Process until smooth. Set pesto aside.

TO PREPARE PASTA: Using a mandoline or vegetable peeler, cut yellow squashes and zucchini into long, narrow ribbons (stem to blossom ends). Heat a large nonstick frying pan over medium heat. Coat pan with nonstick cooking spray. Add shallot and sauté until softened, about 3 minutes. Add yellow squash and zucchini, and season generously with salt and pepper. Sauté until the squashes are just tender, about 8 minutes. Stir in the pesto and heat for 1 minute. Remove from heat and stir in 1 tablespoon of cheese.

Transfer to a warmed serving dish and toss with remaining Asiago cheese. Serve hot. Makes 3 to 4 servings.

Marinated and Grilled Zucchini

2 Tbs. white wine or champagne vinegar
2 Tbs. fresh lemon juice
2 cloves garlic, minced
2 tsp. chopped fresh thyme leaves
Kosher salt and black pepper
⅓ cup extra virgin olive oil
2 large zucchini
3 Tbs. grated Parmesan cheese

In a small bowl, whisk together vinegar, lemon juice, garlic, and thyme. Season with salt and pepper and gradually whisk in olive oil. Slice zucchini in quarters, longwise, and place into a 13 × 9 glass baking dish. Pour all but 2 tablespoons of marinade over zucchini, and toss to coat. Then cover and marinate at room temperature for 2 to 6 hours. Grill zucchini on outdoor barbecue or indoor grill pan until they are crisp, tender, and brown, turning occasionally for about 8 minutes.

Transfer zucchini to a serving platter and drizzle with reserved 2 tablespoons of marinade. Add grated Parmesan cheese. Serve hot or at room temperature.

Parmesan Peppers

4 bell peppers (mix of yellow, red, and orange)
2 Tbs. olive oil
1 garlic clove, thinly sliced
6 sprigs of thyme
Kosher salt
Freshly ground black pepper
¼ cup grated Parmesan cheese
2 Tbs. lemon juice

Preheat oven to 425°F. Stem, core, and quarter bell peppers; place on a baking sheet. Toss with olive oil, garlic, and thyme sprigs; season with salt and freshly ground black pepper. Arrange skin side down in a single layer and roast in oven until softened, about 10 minutes. Remove the peppers from the oven, top with Parmesan, and broil until cheese is melted and peppers are slightly charred. Sprinkle lemon juice over peppers before serving. Serves 4.

Green Beans with Lemon and Almonds

2 oz. sliced almonds
1 lb. green beans, trimmed
1 Tbs. butter
Juice of ½ lemon
Salt and pepper to taste

In a medium-size skillet, toast almonds over medium heat, about 1 to 2 minutes. Remove almonds from skillet and add ½ inch water to pan. Bring water to boil, add beans and cover. Reduce heat. Cook beans 4 to 5 minutes or until tender yet still green. Drain beans and set aside. Return pan to stovetop and melt butter over moderate heat. Add lemon juice and beans to butter and coat evenly. Season with salt and pepper, to taste. Transfer green beans to serving plate and top with almonds. Makes 3 to 4 servings.

Angie's Corn Sauté

6 cups fresh corn, cut from the cob (12 ears)
4 Tbs. butter
¼ to ½ cup diced sweet onion
2 Tbs. water
Salt and white pepper to taste
4 Tbs. whipped cream

Slice kernels off of corn cobs. Using the back of a knife, press hard on the empty ears of corn to extract the "milky" substance from cobs. Melt butter in a large skillet. Add onions and sauté for 2 to 4 minutes, until soft. Add corn and water. Sauté for 8 minutes over medium-low heat. Season to taste with salt and pepper. Add cream at the end and continue to cook about 2 minutes or until cream is warm. Makes 10 to 12 servings.

Corn, Okra, and Tomatoes

1 large onion, chopped
1 large green bell pepper, chopped
2 garlic cloves, minced
6 Tbs. butter
2 cups chopped plum tomatoes
2½ cups fresh corn, cut from the cob (about 5 ears)
1 cup sliced, fresh or frozen okra
1 tsp. salt
½ tsp. freshly ground black pepper

Cook first 3 ingredients in butter in a skillet over medium-high heat, stirring constantly, until tender. Add tomato; bring to a low boil. Reduce heat and simmer, uncovered, 15 minutes. Add corn and remaining ingredients, bring to boil. Reduce heat and simmer 9 minutes or until corn is tender. Salt and pepper to taste. Makes 4 to 5 servings.

Juanita's Fresh Corn Pudding

2 cups fresh corn, cut from cob (about 4 ears)
2 tsp. salt
2 Tbs. flour
1 Tbs. granulated sugar
3 large eggs, well-beaten
1 cup milk
3 Tbs. butter, melted

Preheat oven to 350°F. Cut corn off of cob and place in small bowl; set aside. In a medium bowl, mix salt, flour, and sugar well. Add eggs, milk, and butter. Stir together. Mix in corn. Combine well. Pour mixture into a well-buttered 8 × 8 baking dish. Bake for 50 to 60 minutes or until set in the center. Makes 3 to 4 servings.

Grilled Corn Out of the Husk with Lime Butter

6 ears of corn, husks and silks removed
Cooking spray
2 Tbs. softened butter
1 tsp. lime zest
½ tsp. kosher salt
¼ tsp. ground red pepper

Preheat grill to medium-high heat. Spray each ear with cooking spray. Place corn on grill over direct heat for 12 minutes, turning every 2 to 3 minutes. Dark char spots will appear on the cobs. Combine butter, zest, salt, and red pepper in a small bowl and serve with corn.

Corn O'Brien

4 Tbs. butter

5 cups fresh corn, cut from cob (about 10 ears)

½ cup red bell pepper, diced

½ cup green bell pepper, diced

½ cup sweet onions, diced

1 cup water

Salt and pepper to taste

Melt butter in a large skillet. Add corn, peppers, and onions with 1 cup of water. Bring to a low boil. Stir frequently for 5 minutes.

Serve immediately or pour corn onto a rimmed sheet pan to cool. Once cooled, freeze corn in plastic quart freezer bags.

TO DEFROST CORN: Place corn in a microwave-safe container. Microwave on medium heat 6 to 8 minutes or until hot. Makes 4 to 6 servings.

From Our Family Album

One of Aunt Juanita's summer traditions was to make plenty of Corn O'Brien during the peak of corn season. Many cousins were involved in shucking the corn to prepare for this delicious recipe.

ENTRÉES

— *From Our Family Album* —

For generations, Eckert family meals have included the freshest ingredients from the farm. Suppertime has often brought together friends and family after a full day of harvest and sales. Today, we still celebrate meals together and we firmly believe the best memories are made around the dinner table.

Pork Tenderloin with Balsamic Peaches

1 pork tenderloin (about 1 lb.), silver skin removed

3-4 rosemary sprigs, leaves removed from stem

Black pepper and salt to taste

2 Tbs. butter, divided

2 fresh peaches, quatered and peeled

2 Tbs. aged balsamic (white or dark) vinegar

1 Tbs. olive oil

Place pork tenderloin on a sheet of plastic wrap or butcher paper. Spread rosemary and pepper on pork. Wrap pork in plastic wrap or butcher paper and place in refrigerator for 1 to 2 hours. Preheat oven to 375°F. Remove pork from refrigerator and allow it to come to room temperature, about 30 to 40 minutes. Remove rosemary leaves and dispose. Salt pork. Add 1 tablespoon butter and 1 tablespoon olive oil to a large stainless steel skillet on high heat. Brown each side of tenderloin for 2 to 3 minutes. Remove pork and place in an oven-safe dish. Bake pork until it reaches an internal temperature of 135°F (approximately 20 minutes).

Meanwhile, over medium heat, add the other tablespoon of butter to the stainless steel skillet. Place peaches in the skillet. Sauté peaches for 2 minutes per side for a total of 6 minutes. Turn heat to low and add 2 tablespoons balsamic vinegar. Let the sauce reduce by ⅔, about 3 to 4 minutes. Place peaches and sauce in a small bowl. Serve pork and warm peaches together. Makes about 4 servings.

Baked Ribs with Spicy Blackberry Sauce

4 tsp. chili powder

4 garlic cloves, minced

1 tsp. salt

2 slabs baby back pork ribs (about 2 lbs. each)

2½ cups fresh blackberries, washed and drained

½ cup ketchup

½ cup Eckert's Pure Honey

½ cup fresh, peeled ginger, minced

2 Tbs. balsamic vinegar (white or dark)

2 tsp. hot pepper sauce

Salt and black pepper to taste

Preheat oven to 400°F. Mix chili powder, garlic, and salt in a small bowl. Rub mixture into ribs. Place ribs on a large baking sheet, meaty side up. Bake ribs for 50 minutes.

Purée remaining ingredients in a blender until almost smooth. Cook purée over medium-high heat until reduced to 1 cup, stirring frequently for about 5 minutes. Season sauce to taste with salt and pepper. Brush ribs with enough sauce to coat. Continue baking until sauce browns and forms a thick glaze. Cut slabs between bones into individual ribs. Serve with remaining blackberry sauce. Serves 4.

Fresh Tomato Pasta

4-6 tomatoes, chopped
5 Tbs. extra virgin olive oil
2 tsp. fresh lemon juice
⅓ cup chopped, fresh basil
Salt and pepper to taste
1 lb. spaghetti or fettuccine pasta
½ cup grated Parmesan cheese

Mix together tomatoes, oil, lemon juice, basil, and salt and pepper; set aside. Bring large pot of salted water to a boil and add pasta, cook until al dente according to package directions. Drain pasta and immediately toss with tomato mixture; sprinkle with cheese and serve at once. Makes 4 to 6 servings.

Peach Pork Kabobs

1 Tbs. chili powder
2 Tbs. olive oil
1 lb. pork tenderloin, silver skin removed
1 green bell pepper, seeded
½ red onion
2 firm peaches, peeled or unpeeled
Wooden skewers
Eckert's Peach Salsa or recipe on page 81

Combine chili powder and olive oil; stir to blend and set aside. Cut meat, vegetables, and peaches into 1-inch cubes, toss with seasoned olive oil and chill for 30 minutes. Soak skewers in warm water for 30 minutes to prevent burning on the grill. Alternate ingredients on skewers; grill over medium heat for 10 to 12 minutes, turning once or twice. Serve hot with Amish Peach Salsa. Makes 5 to 6 servings.

Family Favorite Grill Bundles

1 tsp. onion salt

¼ tsp. pepper

½ tsp. granulated garlic

½ lb. hamburger, browned

½ cup potatoes, unpeeled, uncooked, cut into ¼-inch cubes

½ cup fresh corn, uncooked, cut from the cob (1 ear)

½ cup carrots, cut into ½-inch pieces

½ cup fresh green beans, trimmed

½ cup shredded cheddar cheese, optional

8 (9-inch) squares heavy-duty foil

Preheat grill or oven to 375°F. Create a seasoning mix by combining onion salt, pepper, and garlic. Set aside. Combine hamburger, potatoes, corn, carrots, and green beans with 1 teaspoon of the seasoning mix. Spoon equal portions onto the center of each foil square. Seal. Grill 35 to 40 minutes. If desired, open bundle after baking and add cheese. Reseal to allow cheese to melt. Makes 8 servings.

From Our Farm

If green bell peppers are left on the plant, they will turn red and can be harvested as red peppers.

Peach Pork Chops

1 Tbs. vegetable oil
4 boneless pork chops, 1 inch thick
¾ tsp. salt, divided
½ tsp. pepper, divided
½ cup chicken broth
½ cup Eckert's Peach Preserves
2 cups peeled, sliced peaches
¼ tsp. ground ginger
1 Tbs. Eckert's Honey Mustard
1 Tbs. apple cider vinegar

Heat oil in a large stainless steel sauté pan over medium-high heat. Season the pork chops with ½ teaspoon salt and ¼ teaspoon pepper. Place the pork chops in a single layer in the pan and brown for two minutes per side. Remove the pork chops from the pan and set aside. Add the broth and cook over high heat, scraping up browned bits from the pan. Reduce the heat to low.

Place peach preserves, peaches, ginger, honey mustard, vinegar, remaining ¼ teaspoon salt, and ¼ teaspoon pepper in the pan and stir to combine. Return the pork to the pan and baste with the peach mixture. Cover the pan and simmer for 15 minutes or until the internal temperature of the pork reaches 140°F.

Bacon, Peach, and Arugula Sandwiches with Pesto Mayo

8 slices Eckert's thick-sliced bacon
¼ cup fresh basil
2 Tbs. olive oil
1 tsp. fresh lemon juice
¼ tsp. kosher salt
Fresh ground pepper
3 Tbs. mayonnaise
8 slices of Eckert's Hummingbird Bread or whole-grain bread
2 peaches, pitted and sliced
2 cups baby arugula, washed and dried

Cook bacon in a large skillet over medium heat. Turn a few times until bacon is crisp, 8 to 10 minutes. Transfer bacon to a paper towel-lined plate and allow to cool. Cut bacon slices in half. In a food processor, pulse basil, olive oil, lemon juice, 1 teaspoon water, salt, and a few grinds of black pepper until smooth. Add mayonnaise and pulse until well combined. Toast bread and spread evenly with basil mayonniase. Divide peaches, bacon, and arugula among four of the slices of bread. Top with remaining bread slices. Makes 4 sandwiches.

Fried Green Tomato and Bacon Sandwich

3 large green tomatoes
Kosher salt
½ large sweet onion, thinly sliced
8 oz. goat cheese, crumbled
Freshly milled black pepper
⅓ cup yellow cornmeal
2 Tbs. extra virgin olive oil
1 large garlic clove, sliced
Mayonnaise
12 slices of cooked bacon
8 slices Eckert's Country White Bread, toasted

Trim off and discard a thin slice from each end of the tomatoes. Cut each tomato into 4 slices, about ½-inch thick. Sprinkle the slices on both sides with salt, using about ½ teaspoon total; drain in a colander 10 minutes. Pat the tomato slices dry, season with pepper, and dip in cornmeal to coat on both sides. Heat the oil and garlic in a large skillet over medium heat until hot and the garlic just starts to turn golden brown. Remove the garlic and discard. Pour off half of the seasoned oil in a small dish and reserve. Increase the heat to medium-high and brown half the tomato slices on both sides, about 5 minutes total. Repeat with reserved oil and tomatoes. Spread mayonnaise on toasted bread. Top with bacon, onion, goat cheese, fried tomatoes, and remaining bread. Slice each sandwich in half and serve.

Golden Chicken
with Bell Pepper and Tomato

2 Tbs. olive oil

4 boneless, skinless chicken breast halves

½ tsp. kosher salt

¼ tsp. freshly ground black pepper

1 medium onion, thinly sliced

1 orange or red bell pepper, cored and sliced into strips

1 pint cherry or grape tomatoes, halved

3 cloves garlic, minced

¾ cup dry white wine or chicken stock

¼ cup chopped fresh parsley

Heat oil in a large skillet over medium heat. Season chicken with salt and pepper and cook until medium brown on both sides, 4 to 5 minutes per side. Transfer chicken to a plate. Add onion to skillet and cook, stirring occasionally until soft, 4 to 5 minutes. Add tomatoes and peppers and cook for 2 more minutes, stirring frequently. Add garlic and cook 2 more minutes. Return chicken to the skillet and pour in wine. Simmer until chicken is cooked through and sauce has thickened slightly, about 5 minutes or until the internal temperature of the thickest part of the breast reads 165°F. Top with parsley before serving.

Ribeye Steaks with Grilled Corn Salsa

GRILLED CORN SALSA
1 cup fresh corn (2 ears, grilled)

2 Tbs. + 1 tsp. olive oil

2 Tbs. balsamic vinegar (white or dark)

½ tsp. Dijon mustard

¼ tsp. kosher salt

⅛ tsp. freshly ground black pepper

½ cup tomatoes, finely diced

⅓ cup cucumbers, peeled and finely diced

¼ cup basil leaves, thinly sliced

RIBEYE STEAKS
4 (10 oz.) ribeye steaks (1½-inch thickness)

2 Tbs. canola oil, in a small glass bowl

Kosher salt

Fresh ground pepper

TO PREPARE CORN SALSA: Lightly brush corn with 1 teaspoon of olive oil. Grill corn over direct-medium heat (400-450°F) with lid closed, until lightly charred and tender, turning occasionally. Set aside and cool. Cut kernels from cob. In medium bowl, whisk together 2 tablespoons olive oil, vinegar, mustard, salt, and pepper. Add tomatoes, cucumbers, and corn. Stir well. Gently incorporate basil into salsa and allow to rest at room temperature while preparing ribeyes.

TO PREPARE RIBEYES: Lightly brush steaks with oil. Sprinkle both sides with salt and pepper. Allow steaks to stand at room temperature for 50 minutes before grilling. Before turning on grill, dip paper towel in remaining oil and use tongs to oil the grates of the grill to prevent sticking. Grill steaks over high heat, flipping once, until cooked to desired doneness. For medium rare, place steaks on grill for 2 minutes, turn 45 degrees and cook for another 2 minutes. Flip steaks and cook for another 2 minutes. Reduce heat to low and turn steaks 45 degrees for final 2 minutes. Let steaks stand 2 to 3 minutes before cutting. Top with corn salsa.

Chicken Kabobs with Summer Vegetables

1½ lb. skinless, boneless chicken breasts, cut into 2-inch pieces
½ cup plain yogurt, regular or Greek
¼ cup chopped green onions
1 large clove garlic, minced
½ cup fresh cilantro, chopped
2 Tbs. olive oil
½ tsp. kosher salt
¼ tsp. fresh cracked pepper
1 medium zucchini
2 cups (1 pint) cherry tomatoes
Bamboo skewers

In a glass bowl, combine chicken, yogurt, green onion, garlic, cilantro, oil, salt, and pepper. Mix well. Cover and refrigerate at least 2 hours or as long as overnight. Soak bamboo skewers (8 to 10) in water for at least 20 minutes. Cut zucchini in half, lengthwise. Then cut into 2-inch thick slices. Thread chicken, zucchini, and tomatoes on skewers. Discard remaining chicken marinade. Grill kabobs on clean grates over medium-high heat for 8 minutes. Turn and grill another 8 minutes. Serve immediately. Makes 4 servings.

Summer Harvest Pizza

1 medium summer squash, cut crosswise into 1-inch-thick slices

1 medium zucchini, cut crosswise into 1-inch-thick slices

1 large red bell pepper, quartered and seeded

2 Tbs. olive oil

3 garlic cloves, minced

1 lb. refrigerated pizza dough or homemade dough (see recipe on facing page)

2 Tbs. cornmeal

⅔ cup pizza sauce

Salt

Freshly ground black pepper

1 cup shredded fontina cheese

¼ cup basil leaves, julienned

2 tsp. fresh thyme leaves

If using refrigerated dough, remove dough from refrigerator. Let stand covered for 1 hour or until dough comes to room temperature.

Oil grates on grill. Preheat grill to high heat. Brush summer squash, zucchini, and bell pepper with 2 tablespoons oil. Grill squash and zucchini 3 minutes on each side or until tender, set aside to cool. Place pepper quarters, skin side down, on grill rack and grill for 6 minutes or until blistered. Place peppers in a zip-top plastic bag; seal. Let stand 10 minutes, then peel blackened skin. Coarsely chop squash, zucchini, and pepper and add garlic. Toss to combine.

On a lightly floured baking sheet sprinkled with cornmeal, press or roll the pizza dough out to a 14-inch circle. Crimp edges to form a ½-inch border.

Place pizza dough on a perforated pizza pan, cornmeal side up, on grill and grill for 4 minutes or until blistered. Turn dough over; grill 3 minutes. Remove from grill. Spread pizza sauce evenly over top side of crust. Arrange vegetable mixture evenly over sauce; sprinkle evenly with salt and black pepper to taste. Top with cheese. Return pizza to grill rack, and grill for 4 to 6 minutes or until thoroughly cooked. Sprinkle with fresh herbs and cut into slices.

Homemade Pizza Dough

1 cup warm water (100°F), divided
2 cups + 2 Tbs. all-purpose flour
1 package dry yeast (about 2¼ tsp.)
4 tsp. olive oil, divided
½ tsp. kosher salt, divided

Pour ¾ cup warm water in the bowl of a stand mixer with dough hook attached. Weigh or lightly spoon flour into dry measuring cups and spoons; level with a knife. Add flour to ¾ cup water; mix until combined. (If dough is too sticky, add 1 tablespoon of flour.) Cover and let stand 20 minutes. Combine remaining ¼ cup water and yeast in a small bowl; let stand 5 minutes or until bubbly. Add yeast mixture, 4 teaspoons oil, and ½ teaspoon salt to flour mixture; mix 5 minutes or until a soft dough forms. Place dough in a large bowl coated with cooking spray; cover surface of dough with plastic wrap lightly coated with cooking spray. Refrigerate up to 24 hours or use immediately.

--- *From Our Kitchen* ---

For a baked pizza, preheat oven to 425°F. Brush a jelly roll pan or round pizza pan with 1 tablespoon of olive oil and sprinkle with 2 tablespoons of corn meal. Press dough to edges and crimp a ½-inch border around the pan. Top as desired and bake for 35 to 40 minutes or until crust is firm.

Bow-Tie Pasta with Fresh Vegetables

8 oz. uncooked bow-tie pasta
1 large sweet onion, diced
3 Tbs. olive oil
3 garlic cloves, minced
2 medium zucchini, chopped
2 cups diced tomatoes
2 medium yellow squash, chopped
1 cup fresh corn, cut from cob (2 ears)
2 Tbs. fresh basil, chopped
½ tsp. salt
½ tsp. fresh ground pepper
1 cup freshly grated Parmesan cheese

Cook bow-tie pasta in large pot of boiling water according to package directions. Drain; keep warm. Meanwhile, sauté onion in oil in large saucepan over medium heat until softened. Add garlic; cook 1 minute or until fragrant. Add zucchini and squash; cook 6 to 8 minutes or until soft. Add tomatoes, corn, basil, salt, and pepper; cook 7 to 10 minutes or until vegetables are crisp-tender. In large bowl, toss bow-tie pasta with sauce and ½ cup Parmesan cheese. Serve sprinkled with remaining ½ cup cheese. Makes 4 servings.

DESSERTS

—— *From Our Family Album* ——

Baking from scratch with the freshest ingredients
was always Grandma Ella Eckert's way. Of course,
living on top of a hill surrounded by apple and
peach orchards and having chickens in the
backyard made that easy. Every Saturday it was
Grandma's ritual to make coffee cakes, pies, and
homemade egg noodles.

Peaches and Cream Pie

1 (9-inch) unbaked pie shell
2 cups peeled and sliced peaches
3 large eggs, divided
⅓ cup heavy cream
⅔ cup granulated sugar, divided
1 (8 oz.) package cream cheese, softened
2 tsp. fresh lemon juice

Partially bake pie shell at 400°F for 8 to 10 minutes; remove from oven and allow to cool. Reduce oven temperature to 375°F. Arrange peaches evenly in pie shell. In medium mixing bowl, combine 2 eggs, cream, and ⅓ cup sugar; beat until blended, about 2 to 3 minutes. Pour mixture over peaches. In same mixing bowl add cream cheese, remaining sugar, 1 egg, and lemon juice. Beat until smooth and creamy, about 3 to 4 minutes. Pour mixture evenly over top of peaches and cream mixture. Bake at 375°F for 30 to 40 minutes. Cool. Cover and refrigerate until serving time. Makes 6 servings.

Classic Double Crust Fresh Peach Pie

¾ cup + 1 tsp. granulated sugar

⅓ cup flour, or as needed

5-6 cups peeled and ¼-inch sliced peaches

2 Tbs. cold butter, cut into small pieces

½ to 1 tsp. flavorings* of choice or to taste

2 (9-inch) unbaked homemade or frozen pie crusts, defrosted

1 tsp. milk or water to brush on top crust

Preheat oven to 400°F. In a 4-quart mixing bowl, combine sugar and flour. Add prepared peaches and flavoring. Mix gently to thoroughly cover all the peaches. Spread prepared peaches in unbaked pie crust. Randomly add cold pieces of butter. Cover with top pie crust. Seal edges by lightly moistening the edge of the bottom pie shell with water. Flute. Prick top crust with fork to vent pie while baking. A lattice-style top crust is another choice.

Place pie in preheated oven and bake about 30 to 35 minutes. Remove from oven and brush a teaspoon of milk or water on top. Sprinkle with remaining 1 teaspoon of sugar. Continue to bake another 15 to 20 minutes. If edges are browning too quickly, cover edges with foil. Allow pie to cool about 1 hour for easier cutting.

Frozen or fresh peaches can be used for this recipe. If frozen peaches are used, defrost until peaches are defrosted but still cold and holding their shape. About 45 minutes to 1 hour. Add 10 to 15 minutes to the first baking time.

Makes 6 servings.

*FLAVORING SUGGESTIONS: ground cinnamon and nutmeg, lemon juice, or almond extract.

HINT: Remove frozen pie shell from aluminum pie pan. Place shell in 9-inch glass pie plate. Gently press to fit plate.

If you like a thicker filling because peaches are extra juicy, use another 1 to 2 tablespoons flour.

Fresh Peach Custard Pie

3 cups peeled and sliced peaches
1 (9-inch) unbaked pie shell
2 large eggs, beaten
⅔ cup granulated sugar
¼ tsp. salt
2 Tbs. flour
½ cup light cream or milk
½ tsp. vanilla extract

Preheat oven to 400°F. Arrange peaches evenly in bottom of pie shell. In a mixing bowl combine eggs, sugar, salt, and flour; add cream or milk and vanilla. Stir until smooth. Pour mixture over peaches. Bake for 10 minutes; reduce oven temperature to 375°F and bake for an additional 30 to 40 minutes or until knife inserted in center comes out clean. Cover and refrigerate. Makes 6 servings.

—— From Our Family Album ——

We have more dessert recipes for summer than any other season! However, the absolute Eckert family favorite is the Fresh Peach Custard Pie. Sometimes we substitute blackberries for peaches or include a combination of blackberries and peaches.

Grammy's Peach Cake

CAKE

1 cup flour
½ tsp. baking powder
½ cup granulated sugar
⅛ tsp. salt
2 Tbs. butter, cold
1 large egg, beaten
1-2 Tbs. milk
6-7 peaches, peeled and sliced

TOPPING

½ cup sugar
¼ tsp. ground nutmeg
1 tsp. cornstarch
¼ tsp. ground cinnamon
1 Tbs. butter cut into small pieces

TO PREPARE CAKE: Preheat oven to 375°F. In large mixing bowl, sift flour, baking powder, sugar, and salt together; cut in butter with knife until mixture is crumbly. Stir in egg and milk and mix well. Spread in greased 8 × 8 baking pan. Cover with peaches.

TO PREPARE TOPPING: In a small bowl, combine ingredients for topping and mix well. Sprinkle mixture over peaches; dot with butter. Bake for 30 to 40 minutes. Makes 9 servings.

NOTE: You can substitute 1 to 3 cups frozen sliced peaches for fresh ones. Thaw before using and drain well. Pat dry with paper towel to absorb excess moisture.

Peachy Pound Cake

1 cup butter, softened

2 cups + 2 Tbs. granulated sugar, divided

4 large eggs

1 tsp. vanilla extract

3 cups flour, divided

1 tsp. baking powder

½ tsp. salt

2 cups peeled and ½-inch chopped peaches

Preheat oven to 325°F. Butter a 10-inch tube pan (angel food cake pan) and coat with 2 tablespoons sugar. In a large bowl with electric mixer, cream together the butter and remaining sugar until light and fluffy, about 3 to 4 minutes. Add eggs one at a time, beating well with each addition; stir in vanilla. Sift together 2¾ cups flour, baking powder, and salt. Gradually stir into the creamed mixture. Coat chopped peaches with remaining ¼ cup flour; fold peaches into batter. Spread batter evenly into prepared pan. Bake for 60 to 70 minutes or until a toothpick inserted toward center comes out clean. Allow cake to cool in pan for 10 minutes before inverting onto wire rack to cool completely. Makes 10 to 12 servings.

Peach Upside-Down Cake

CAKE
⅓ cup shortening
⅔ cup granulated sugar
⅔ cup milk
1 tsp. vanilla extract
2 large eggs
2 tsp. baking powder
1⅔ cups flour
⅛ tsp. salt
¼ tsp. almond extract

PEACH MIXTURE
⅓ cup butter
1 cup light brown sugar
1½ cups sliced peaches

Preheat oven to 350°F. With electric mixer, cream shortening and sugar until light and fluffy, about 2 minutes. Add next seven ingredients and beat well. Set aside. Place butter and brown sugar in a sheet cake pan. Place pan on stove top burner on medium heat. Stirring constantly over medium heat, dissolve sugar. Turn off heat. Add peaches. Stir to coat peaches. Pour in cake batter and bake for 40 to 45 minutes. Allow to cool 5 to 10 minutes. With knife to loosen around edges, turn cake over onto large serving platter, peach side up. Serve hot or cold with whipped cream. Makes 6 to 8 servings.

Grandma Ruth's Peach Cake

1 Tbs. butter, softened
2-3 peaches, peeled and sliced
1 cup granulated sugar, divided
2 large eggs
½ cup flour
1 tsp. baking powder
½ cup boiling water
Whipped cream (garnish)

Preheat oven to 350°F. Butter 8 × 8 glass baking dish. Arrange peaches in prepared baking pan and sprinkle peaches with ¼ cup sugar. In mixing bowl with electric mixer, beat eggs until very light, about 6 to 8 minutes; add remaining sugar 1 tablespoon at a time, beating after each addition. Stir in flour and baking powder. Gradually add water and mix well. Pour batter over peaches. Bake for 35 minutes; do not remove from pan while cooling. May be served warm or cool. When ready to serve, cut into 6 pieces and turn to see peaches. Top with whipped cream. Makes 6 servings. This recipe can be doubled and put into a 9 × 13 glass pan.

Fresh Peach Custard Tart

5 cups peeled and cubed or sliced peaches, divided
⅔ cup sugar
3 Tbs. + 2 tsp. cornstarch
1 cup water
1 Tbs. lemon juice
1 Tbs. butter
1 (9-inch) pie crust, baked in tart pan, cooled

CUSTARD
1¼ cups milk
2 large egg yolks, beaten
¼ cup granulated sugar
1 Tbs. butter
½ tsp. vanilla extract

In a 3-quart saucepan, stir together 1½ cups of peaches, ⅔ cup sugar, 3 tablespoons cornstarch, and water. Bring to a boil over high heat, stirring constantly. Cook 2 minutes or until very thick. Stir in lemon juice and 1 tablespoon butter. Remove from heat and cool 15 minutes. Drain remaining peaches and stir into cooked peach mixture. Transfer mixture to baked crust. Refrigerate until chilled.

TO PREPARE CUSTARD: In 2-quart saucepan, mix together milk, egg yolks, sugar, and butter. Cook and stir over medium heat until mixture boils and thickens, about 2 minutes. Stir in vanilla. Transfer custard to shallow dish and cover surface with plastic wrap. Refrigerate 2 hours. Spread cooled custard over peaches. Refrigerate tart at least 3 hours to set.

Makes 6 to 8 servings.

—— *From Our Family Album* ——

Because every dessert is even better with Eckert's Frozen Custard, multiple quarts of custard can be found in our family freezers throughout the year.

Peach and Blackberry Cobbler with Streusel Topping

COBBLER

4 cups peaches, peeled and sliced

2 cups blackberries, rinsed and dried

⅔ cup flour

1¾ cups sugar

¼ tsp. cinnamon

5 eggs

1 tsp. vanilla

2 cups milk

½ cup heavy cream

TOPPING

1 cup flour

⅔ cup granulated sugar

⅔ cup butter, slightly cold

1 tsp. vanilla extract

TO PREPARE COBBLER: Preheat oven to 375°F. Mix peaches and berries and put in buttered 13 × 9 baking dish. In mixing bowl, combine all remaining ingredients and beat until smooth. Pour mixture over fruit and bake 30 minutes. Remove from oven.

TO PREPARE TOPPING: In small bowl, combine flour and sugar. Cut in butter until mixture is crumbly; add vanilla and toss to mix. Sprinkle cake mixture over cobbler, return to oven and bake an additional 15 to 20 minutes or until cake mixture is brown and knife inserted into center comes out clean.

Makes 8 to 10 servings.

Fresh Peach Glacé Pie

1 cup granulated sugar
3 Tbs. cornstarch
½ cup water
Juice of ½ lemon
4½ to 5 cups peeled and sliced peaches, divided
1 (9-inch) baked pie shell
Whipped cream (garnish)
3 oz. package cream cheese (optional)

In a 3-quart saucepan, combine sugar and cornstarch; stir in water, lemon juice, and 2½ cups peaches. Cook on medium heat, stirring, about 8 to 10 minutes until peaches are slightly soft. Allow mixture to cool about 30 minutes. Fill pie shell with remaining peaches and pour cooked mixture over top. Chill for several hours. Top with dollops of whipped cream and serve. Makes 6 servings.

NOTE: You may spread one 3 oz. package of softened cream cheese over bottom of pie shell before filling.

From Our Kitchen

To bake an empty pie crust, also known as blind bake, prick the sides and bottom of the crust with a fork several times. Place on a cookie sheet and fill the shell with pie weights or dried beans. Bake according to package directions or about 15 minutes at 400°F. Cool before filling.

Peach Cobbler with Pie Crust Top

5 cups peaches, peeled and sliced
1 cup granulated sugar
3 Tbs. flour
½ tsp. ground cinnamon
1 Tbs. butter
1 (9-inch) unbaked pie shell
Whipped cream, Eckert's Frozen Custard, or heavy cream

Preheat oven to 425°F. In a large mixing bowl, combine peaches, sugar, flour, and cinnamon and mix gently. Pour into 8- or 9-inch deep dish pie plate. Dot top with butter. Top mixture with pie crust. Bake for 35 minutes; allow to cool. Serve topped with whipped cream, Eckert's Frozen Custard, or heavy cream. Makes 6 servings.

Magic Peach Cobbler

½ cup butter
1 cup granulated sugar, divided
1 cup flour
1½ tsp. baking powder
¾ cup milk
2½ to 3 cups peaches, peeled and sliced
Whipped cream or Eckert's Frozen Custard

Preheat oven to 350°F. Place butter in 13 × 9 baking dish and melt in oven. In a bowl, combine ½ cup sugar, flour, baking powder, and milk; mix well. Pour mixture evenly over melted butter; do not stir! Arrange peaches on top of batter in rows to cover buttered bottom of dish; sprinkle with remaining sugar. Bake for 35 minutes or until golden and bubbly. Serve topped with whipped cream or Eckert's Frozen Custard. Makes 10 to 12 servings.

Peach Kuchen

1 cup flour
½ tsp. baking powder
¼ tsp. salt
½ cup butter (1 stick)
¼ cup + 3 Tbs. granulated sugar, divided
1 large egg
1 tsp. vanilla extract
3 cups sliced peaches
3 Tbs. sugar

Preheat oven to 350°F. Grease and flour a 9-inch springform pan. In a bowl, sift together flour, baking powder, and salt and set aside. In a mixing bowl with electric mixer, cream together butter and ¼ cup sugar until light and fluffy, about 2 minutes. Beat in egg and stir in vanilla. Gently stir in flour mixture until dough is formed. Spread dough over the bottom and about 1 inch up the sides of springform pan. Arrange peach slices in a spoke pattern over the dough. Sprinkle top with 3 tablespoons sugar and bake for 35 to 40 minutes or until golden brown. Makes 6 servings.

Peach-Amaretto Bread Pudding

1 loaf Eckert's French bread, torn into 1½-inch to 2-inch pieces
1 qt. half and half (4 cups)
1 Tbs. unsalted butter, softened
3 large eggs, lightly beaten
1½ cups granulated sugar
2 tsp. almond extract
4 to 5 large peaches, peeled and thinly sliced
1 cup sliced almonds

In a large bowl, combine bread and half and half. Cover and chill 1 hour. Preheat oven to 325°F. Grease a 13 × 9 glass baking dish with butter. In a bowl, combine eggs, sugar, and almond extract. Stir well. Add to chilled bread mixture, stirring gently. Fold in peaches and almonds and pour mixture into prepared pan. Bake 1 hour or until set and lightly browned. Let stand 15 minutes before serving with Amaretto Sauce (see below). Makes 10 to 12 servings.

Amaretto Sauce

½ cup butter (1 stick)
1 cup sifted powdered sugar
1 large egg, lightly beaten
¼ cup amaretto

In a 1-quart saucepan, combine butter and sugar and cook until butter melts and sugar dissolves. Gradually stir about ¼ hot mixture into lightly beaten egg. Slowly stir in remaining hot mixture. Cook and stir over medium heat until mixture thickens, about 3 to 4 minutes. Remove from heat. Stir in amaretto. Let cool to room temperature, stirring occasionally. Serve with Bread Pudding (see above). Serves 10 to 12.

Double Crust Fresh Blackberry Pie

1 cup + ½ tsp. granulated sugar
⅓ cup quick cooking (instant) tapioca
¼ tsp. salt
5 cups fresh blackberries, divided
2 (9-inch) unbaked pie shells
1 large egg, beaten

Preheat oven to 400°F. In large saucepan, mash 1 cup blackberries with potato masher. Stir in 1 cup sugar, tapioca, and salt over medium heat. Stir constantly until mixture comes to a gentle boil, 5 to 7 minutes. Remove mixture from heat and stir in remaining blackberries. Pour filling into crust.

On a floured surface, roll second crust until flattened. Place over filling and trim as necessary. Pinch top and bottom crusts together. Cut slits in top of pie crust. Brush egg on crust (not all of egg mixture will be used). Sprinkle remaining ½ teaspoon sugar on crust. Bake on rimmed sheet pan for 30 to 35 minutes or until golden brown. Makes 6 servings.

—— *From Our Kitchen* ——

To keep peaches from browning, fill a bowl with cold water and dissolve 1 tablespoon of ascorbic acid powder or lemon juice in the water. Slice peaches and place slices in the bowl of water immediately after cutting, submerging them completely. Allow peaches to soak for 10 minutes, remove, and pat dry. Use as desired.

Grilled Peach
and Blackberry Dessert Topping

4 large peaches
2 cups (1 pint) blackberries
1 Tbs. brown sugar
2 Tbs. cognac (optional)
Eckert's Frozen Custard

Slice peaches and spread out on sheet of heavy duty aluminum foil. Add blackberries. Sprinkle fruit mixture with brown sugar. Add cognac (optional). Seal aluminum foil tightly and place on a grill over medium heat for 20 minutes. Carefully remove foil and serve over Eckert's Frozen Custard. Makes 4 servings.

Fresh Berry Tart

1 (9-inch) unbaked pie shell
4 cups fresh berries (blackberries and blueberries)
¼ cup granulated sugar
1 Tbs. all-purpose flour
1 tsp. lemon zest
Pinch of salt
1 large egg, beaten
Granulated sugar for sprinkling

Preheat oven to 350°F. Roll out pie crust flat on a floured surface. Crimp edges all the way around crust, forming a 1-inch border. Toss berries with sugar, flour, lemon zest, and salt. Heap berries in center of dough. Brush pie crust sides and edges with beaten egg. Sprinkle sugar on top of berries and crust. Bake tart for 35 minutes or until crust is golden brown. Cut into 6 wedges. Makes 6 servings.

NOTE: Some of the fresh blackberry juices may escape, but that's okay!

Cheesecake-Stuffed Peaches

6 unpeeled medium peaches, halved and pitted

2 Tbs. butter melted

3 Tbs. cinnamon sugar*

4 oz. cream cheese, softened

¼ cup granulated sugar

1 large egg yolk

1½ tsp. vanilla extract

Preheat oven to 350°F. Place a piece of parchment paper over regular-sized muffin pan. Cut an "x" into the paper just above each muffin cup. Dip peach halves, cut side up, in melted butter to coat. Place peach halves, cut side up, in prepared pan. Sprinkle top of peaches with cinnamon-sugar. Set aside. In a medium bowl, beat cream cheese with a mixer on medium speed until smooth, about 1 minute. Add sugar, egg yolk, and vanilla. Beat until combined, about 1 to 2 minutes. Spoon cream cheese mixture into peach centers. Bake, uncovered, about 30 minutes or until lightly browned and softened. Serve warm or at room temperature. Makes 6 servings.

*NOTE: Use a purchased cinnamon-sugar mixture or combine 3 tablespoons granulated sugar with 1 teaspoon ground cinnamon.

Individual Peach Crisp

10 medium peaches, peeled and sliced
¼ cup brown sugar
¾ cup flour
10 (4½-inch) mini pie tins or ramekins

CRUMB TOPPING
2½ cups flour
1⅔ cups brown sugar
1½ tsp. ground cinnamon
1¼ cups quick cooking oats
1¼ cups chilled butter, cut into pieces (2½ sticks)

Preheat oven to 350°F. Combine first 3 ingredients in a large bowl and stir well. Divide peach mixture evenly between greased 4½-inch pie pans or ramekins; set aside. Combine dry ingredients in a medium bowl. Cut in butter with pastry blending tool until crumbly. Divide topping evenly between tins. Place tins on a cookie sheet. Bake for 30 to 35 minutes or until evenly browned. Makes 10 servings.

Eckert's Peach Buttercream Frosting

1 large fresh peach, peeled and chopped
¾ cup butter, softened
1 (32-oz.) package powdered sugar

Process peach in blender or food processor until puréed (purée should measure about ½ cup). Beat butter at medium speed with electric mixter until creamy; gradually add powdered sugar alternately with puréed peach, beating until well blended after peach addition.

Chocolate Zucchini Cake

½ cup butter, softened
⅓ cup vegetable oil
1¾ cups granulated sugar
2 large eggs
1 tsp. vanilla extract
½ cup sour milk*
2¼ cups all-purpose flour
4 Tbs. cocoa powder
½ tsp. baking powder
1 tsp. baking soda
2 cups grated zucchini, unpeeled
⅔ cup mini chocolate chips, divided
26 (4½-inch) mini foil pie tins
Non-stick vegetable cooking spray

Preheat oven to 350°F. With electric mixer, cream butter, oil, and sugar. Add eggs, vanilla, and sour milk. Mix thoroughly. Blend in dry ingredients. Stir in zucchini and ¼ cup chocolate chips. Spoon ¼ cup batter into each greased mini pie tin. Using remaining chocolate chips, sprinkle 4 to 5 chocolate chips on top of each cake. Bake 16 to 17 minutes. Makes 26 servings.

NOTE: The batter can be put into paper-lined muffins cups and baked 22 minutes.

*****TO PREPARE SOUR MILK:** Put ½ tablespoon vinegar with milk to total ½ cup. Let sit 5 minutes.

PRESERVES, SAUCES, & TOPPINGS

Our sweet peaches and crisp apples have been entered in many competitions. Great Grandpa Alvin even won a bronze medal for his fruit display at the 1904 World's Fair in St. Louis. This photo shows our display at the Illinois State Fair in 1953. Times sure have changed since then, but the unparalleled taste and the healthy attributes of fresh Eckert-grown fruit remain the same today.

Peachy BBQ Sauce

1 Tbs. butter
2 shallots, minced
6 peaches, chunked
½ cup Eckert's Peach Butter
3 cups Eckert's Vidalia Onion BBQ
Sauce

In a 2-quart saucepan, heat butter until it melts but do not brown. Add shallots. Cook, stirring often, until translucent. Add peaches, peach butter, and 1 tablespoon water. Cook and stir about 10 minutes or until peaches start to break apart. Simmer 10 minutes; add BBQ sauce. Simmer over low heat, stirring often, to let flavors mingle and peaches dissolve into the sauce. Makes about 5 to 6 cups.

— From Our Family Album —

During peach season, it is our family's pleasure to greet customers, whether it's their first trip to our farms or they have been coming year after year, and we are so delighted when they tell us how much they love our peaches.

Refrigerator Peach Butter

4 to 4½ pounds of peeled peaches
(about 18 medium)
Boiling water
Ice bath
½ cup water
4 cups granulated sugar
6-8 one-cup canning jars with flat
lids and rings

TO PREPARE PULP: Wash and blanch peaches in boiling water for 1 to 3 minutes. Skin will start to crack. Immediately put in ice water. Peel, pit, and slice peaches. Combine peaches and ½ cup water in large saucepan. Simmer until peaches are soft, about 8 to 10 minutes. Purée using a food processor or food mill, being careful not to liquefy. Measure out 8 cups of peach pulp.

TO PREPARE BUTTER: Combine peach pulp and sugar in large saucepan. Cook until thick enough to round up on a spoon, about 30 to 35 minutes. Pour into hot, clean canning jars. Cover, label, and refrigerate up to one month.

--- *From Our Kitchen* ---

To make an ice bath, fill a 5-quart bowl ½ full of crushed or cubed ice. Add cold water to cover ice. Place hot blanched whole peaches in ice-water bath. Slip skins. Discard ice and water.

Refrigerator Bread-n-Butter Pickles

Boiling water

6 pickling cucumbers (about 4 cups, diced)

1 medium white onion, thinly sliced

2 cups (16 fl oz) white wine vinegar

¾ cup granulated sugar

¼ cup kosher or canning salt

1 tsp. celery seeds

1 tsp. mustard seeds

2 bay leaves

1 quart-sized glass canning jar with flat lid and ring

Thoroughly clean quart-sized glass canning jar with lid and ring with hot water and rinse well. Set jar, ring, and lid into medium pan. Pour boiling water over and in jar. Keep hot until ready to use, but do not boil. In stainless steel heat-proof bowl, combine cucumber and onion; set aside. In a small stainless steel saucepan, combine vinegar, sugar, salt, celery seeds, mustard seeds, and bay leaves and bring to a boil over high heat, stirring to dissolve sugar and salt. Immediately pour the vinegar mixture over cucumber and onion slices. Dump hot water from canning jar. Pack hot vegetables and liquid into the jar, discarding any excess liquid. Wipe jar rim with a clean, damp paper towel. Place hot jar lid and ring on clean jar rim. Gently tighten ring. Allow to cool 1 to 2 hours, then immediately refrigerate. The pickles will keep for 1 month. Makes 1 quart.

NOTE: Do not use aluminum pans or bowls for this recipe.

Blackberry Freezer Jam

6 cups (3 pints) fresh blackberries
5 cups granulated sugar
1 cup water
1 package (1¾ ounces) powdered fruit pectin (such as Sure-Jell)

Rinse and drain berries, then place 1 pint at a time in a medium bowl and crush with a potato masher. Transfer crushed berries to another bowl and repeat until you have 3 cups of crushed berries. Pour sugar over berries and stir to mix. Let mixture rest for 15 minutes, stirring occasionally. In a small saucepan, mix 1 cup of water and pectin and bring to a boil over medium-high heat. Boil for 1 minute. Remove pan from heat and pour mixture over berries. Stir well to combine. Divide mixture among 5 freezer-safe containers. Cover containers and let jam set at room temperature for 24 hours, then freeze. Defrost in refrigerator as needed. Makes about 7 cups.

Rosemary Syrup
with Fresh Peaches and Blackberries

¾ cup granulated sugar

¾ cup Gewurztraminer wine

⅓ cup water

3 Tbs. roughly chopped, fresh
rosemary leaves

1 bay leaf

½ tsp. whole peppercorns

3 Tbs. balsamic vinegar

Place all ingredients in a saucepan and bring to a boil. Reduce heat and simmer for 10 minutes. Cool, strain, and store in refrigerator. Serve drizzled over fresh fruit. Makes 8 servings.

NOTE: Gewurztraminer wine is a white wine with the aroma of jasmine, grapefruit, and sandalwood. These fruit-spicy flavors are followed by just a touch of sweetness.

Eckert's Peach Salsa

4 cups diced unpeeled peaches
½ cup red onion, small dice
½ cup green bell pepper, diced small
½ cup red bell pepper, diced small
2-3 Tbs. Eckert's Pure Honey

Place ingredients in medium bowl. Mix all ingredients together. If desired, combine additional flavor ingredients; add to mixture. Adjust seasonings to taste. Cover and chill. For best flavor, allow to come to room temperature about 1 hour before serving.

NOTE: Add a little more heat to this recipe by including 1 teaspoon fresh chopped cilantro and 2 teaspoons of finely chopped fresh jalapeño pepper.

From Our Farm

Eckert's Peach Salsa is an excellent topping for grilled chicken, pork, and white fish. Serve a generous spoonful on a lettuce leaf alongside a main course.

Summer Fruit Salsa

3 cups fresh strawberries, with stems removed and berries chopped

1 large banana, peeled and chopped

1 medium peach, unpeeled and chopped

2 kiwi fruits, peeled and chopped

3 Tbs. lime juice

4 tsp. Eckert's Pure Honey

½ tsp. ground cinnamon

¼ tsp. ground nutmeg

Stir together first 4 ingredients in a big bowl. Mix lime juice and honey and drizzle over fruit; stir gently to coat. Sprinkle cinnamon and nutmeg over fruit; stir gently. Cover with plastic wrap and chill fruit salsa in the refrigerator at least 30 minutes. Serve fruit salsa with Cinnamon Crisps. Makes 2⅔ cups fruit salsa.

Cinnamon Crisps

4 (8-inch) flour tortillas

Vegetable cooking spray

2 Tbs. sugar

¾ tsp. ground cinnamon

Preheat oven to 350°F. Spray one side of each tortilla with vegetable cooking spray. Stir together sugar and cinnamon in small bowl. Sprinkle sugar mixture over each tortilla. Cut tortillas into 8 wedges with pizza cutter. Place about 1 inch apart on an ungreased baking sheet. Bake at 350°F for 6 to 8 minutes or until lightly brown. Remove baking sheet from the oven using oven mitts. Cool. Makes 32 cinnamon crisps.

Homegrown Tomato Salsa

1½ lb. homegrown tomatoes, cored and chopped into ⅓-inch dice

1 large jalapeño pepper, seeds removed, minced fine

½ cup minced red onion

1 clove garlic, minced

¼ cup fresh chopped cilantro

½ tsp. table salt

⅛ tsp. freshly ground pepper

1 tsp. sugar

3 Tbs. lime juice (from 2 medium limes)

Place a large colander in the sink. Add diced tomatoes to colander and allow to drain for 20 to 30 minutes. Shake colander to remove any excess liquid. Pour drained tomatoes into a large bowl, add jalapeño, onion, garlic, and cilantro. Gently incorporate salt, pepper, lime juice, and sugar. Serve immediately.

--- *From Our Farm* ---

For weed control purposes, we plant tomatoes and peppers in soil covered with a thin layer of black plastic. This plastic also allows the sunlight to warm the soil on cool days early in the growing season.

Summer Harvest Corn Salsa

2 Tbs. olive oil

1 Tbs. fresh lime juice

¼ cup chopped, fresh basil

¼ tsp. salt

¼ tsp. pepper

2½ cups fresh corn kernels (about 5 ears), blanched

1 avocado, peeled, diced

2 cups (1 pint) cherry tomatoes, quartered or 1 large tomato, diced, drained

½ cup diced cucumber, peeled

¼ cup finely diced red onion

Eckert's Tortilla Chips

In a large bowl, whisk together olive oil, lime juice, basil, salt, and pepper. Add vegetables and toss to mix. Serve at room temperature with tortilla chips. Makes 12 servings (⅓ cup each).

ECKERT'S
FAMILY HISTORY

Today, the sixth and seventh generations oversee the daily operations of the Eckert farms. The current Eckert orchard business began in 1837 when Johann Peter Eckert landed in Pittsburgh, Pennsylvania, from Dietzenbach, Hesse Darmestadt, Germany, with his wife and four sons. As German tradition would have it, Johann Peter farmed and eventually bought each of his sons a farm. Johann's son Michael followed his instinctive love for the land and lived on the farm we now call Drum Hill, near Fayetteville, Illinois.

The first fruit trees were planted on Michael Eckert's farm in 1862. Michael had three children, but only one son, Henry, lived to adulthood. After his marriage in 1877, Henry built the present Eckert home on Turkey Hill in 1880. The first fruit trees were planted on Turkey Hill in 1890. Henry and Mary Eckert had three sons and a daughter; their daughter died in infancy. Their youngest son, Alvin O., married Ella Heinrich and resided in the family home where they raised three sons, Cornell, Curt, and Vernon.

The Turkey Hill Farm today is what we call our Belleville farm. The first roadside farm stand was opened on Turkey Hill by Alvin O. in 1910 and became the nucleus of our growing business. All three sons majored in agriculture at the University of Illinois and returned home after graduation to turn the business into a father-sons partnership.

Today, Jim Eckert, son of Juanita and Vernon, is president of Eckert Orchards and is the company's chief horticulturist. Lary Eckert, son of Curt and Ruth, recently resigned as president of Eckert's, Inc., after presiding over the company for 30 years. Lary's son, Chris Eckert, succeeded him as president. Chris oversees retail operations, as well as the growing and wholesaling of homegrown products. Additionally, Lary's daughter, Jill Eckert-Tantillo, is vice president of Marketing and Food Services. Angie Eckert, Chris's wife, is vice president of Retail Operations for both the Country Store and the Garden Center.

Index of Recipes